Readers
LEVEL 2

Looking After Me

Going to the Doctor

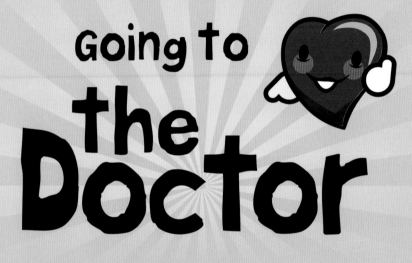

Ian Smith

Quarto
Library

This library edition published in 2015 by Quarto Library.,
an imprint of Quarto Publishing Group USA Inc.
3 Wrigley, Suite A
Irvine, CA 92618

© 2015 QEB Publishing, Published by Quarto Library.,
an imprint of Quarto Publishing Group USA Inc.

Distributed in the United States and Canada by
Lerner Publisher Services
241 First Avenue North
Minneapolis, MN 55401 U.S.A.
www.lernerbooks.com

Library of Congress Cataloging-in-Publication Data

Smith, Ian (Children's author), author.
  Going to the doctor / Ian Smith.
      pages cm. -- (Looking after me. Level 2)
  R130.5.S65 2015
  610--dc23
                              2015010351

ISBN 978 1 93958 181 5

Printed in China

Picture credits
(t=top, b=bottom, l=left, r=right, c=center fc=front cover)

Shutterstock 5t beerkoff, 12b Preto Perola, 15b spflaum, 19c design56, 19b HamsterMan,
24b Preto Perola
Steve Lumb fc, 3b, 4, 6c, 9, 10b, 11t, 11bl, 13b, 14, 16-17, 20-21, 22

Words in **bold** can be found in the Glossary on page 24

Contents

3

I feel sick

I feel sick when I wake up. I am too hot and Mom says that I have a **temperature**.

Mom calls the doctor and makes an **appointment**.

It is my first time going to the doctor. I am a bit worried, but Mom says it will be fine.

The Waiting Room

When we get to the doctor's, we see the receptionist. We tell her we have an appointment.

We have to wait in the waiting room until the doctor can see me.

The receptionist says we won't have to wait long.

The Doctor

When it is my turn to see the doctor, Mom comes with me.

The doctor says hello and tells me her name.

She asks me to sit down.

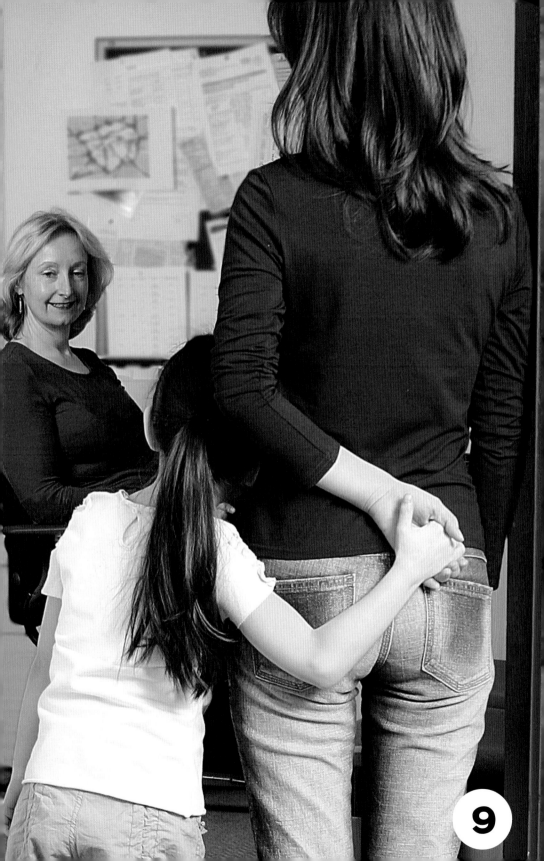

9

The doctor asks what
is wrong with me.
Mom talks to her.

The doctor tells me to
stick out my tongue.
I open my mouth wide
and she looks at
my throat.

"Now I will check your temperature," she says. "I need to see if you have a **fever**."

The doctor uses a **stethoscope** to listen to my chest. She can hear my heart and lungs.

The stethoscope
feels cold on
my skin.

13

The doctor uses a tool
to shine a bright light
into my ear.

She looks into my ear.
It doesn't hurt.

The doctor asks questions about how I feel.

She says I'll be fine but that I need some medicine.

She gives Mom a piece of paper showing the name of the medicine I need.

It is called a **prescription**.

Medicine to Help

The doctor smiles at me.

"Get lots of sleep and take your medicine," she says. "You will feel better soon."

On our way home,
we stop at a pharmacy
to get my medicine.

The bottle has my name
on it. It tells us how I have
to take the medicine.

At home, I put on my pajamas and get into bed.

Mom gives me a spoonful of the medicine. It tastes funny but I swallow it.

In bed, I think about
my trip to the doctor.

She was kind and
she made me feel better.

I think I would like to be a
doctor when I grow up.

Glossary

appointment   a time when you see the doctor

fever   when you are too hot because you are sick

prescription   a piece of paper from the doctor that lists medicine

stethoscope   a tool to listen to noises inside the body

temperature   when you are sick and your head feels hot